USBORNE
CHILDREN'S
PICTURE
ATLAS

Illustrated by Linda Edwards

Written by Ruth Brocklehurst
Designed by Doriana Berkovic

Cartographer: Craig Asquith

Consultants:
Prof. Rex Walford
Dr. Margaret Rostron
Prof. Michael Hitchcock

Contents

The Universe

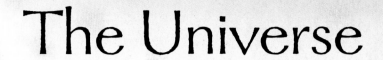

We live in a Universe that's so enormous it's almost impossible to imagine. To picture it, you need to start small, then think big.

A town has streets with houses, shops, schools and other buildings.

Towns and cities

People live in all kinds of places around the world. Most people live in houses or apartments in towns. Really big towns are called cities.

Countries

The land around the world is divided into different countries. Countries usually have towns, cities, farmland and wild countryside.

This small country has towns, fields, mountains and sandy beaches. Not all countries are islands like this one.

Planet Earth

A country is just a small part of the land on the planet Earth. The Earth is a huge ball of rock floating in space. Land covers part of it and the rest is sea.

The Sun is a star. It gives out light and heat.

Mercury

Earth

Venus

Jupiter

Mars

Uranus

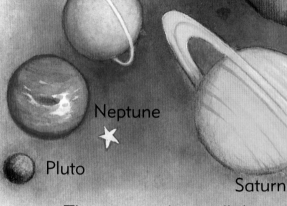

Neptune

Pluto

Saturn

This picture shows all the planets in the Solar System, and Pluto, which scientists now call a dwarf planet.

The Solar System

The Earth is one of nine planets that go around the Sun. Together, the Sun and these planets are called the Solar System. The Earth is the only planet where people, plants and animals live.

The Universe

There are trillions of stars shining in space and the Sun is one of them. A large group of stars is called a galaxy. The Sun belongs to a galaxy called the Milky Way. All the galaxies in space make up the Universe.

On a clear night, you can see thousands of stars.

5

What are maps?

Maps are pictures that show places as they look from above. They usually make places look much smaller than they really are. A book, like this one, full of maps is called an atlas.

Spacecraft called satellites are used to take photographs of the Earth from space.

This is a satellite photograph. It shows part of London.

Making maps

Mapmakers often use photographs of places taken from above to help them draw maps. They also measure the ground to find out the sizes of places and how far they are from each other.

What maps show

When mapmakers draw maps, they just include the important details. Maps often have shading, labels and little pictures to tell you more about a place.

This is a picture map of the same place as the photograph above.

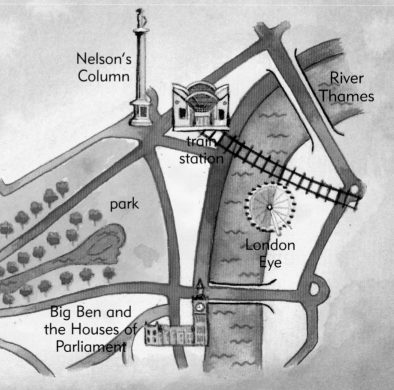

Nelson's Column

River Thames

train station

park

London Eye

Buckingham Palace

Big Ben and the Houses of Parliament

The round Earth

Because the Earth is a ball shape, a photograph can only show one side of it. Mapmakers can show the whole Earth, as it actually looks, by making a model of it. A model Earth is called a globe.

This satellite photograph shows one side of the Earth from space.

If the surface of a globe could be peeled off, this is how it would look.

Peeled Earth

To make a flat map of the round Earth, mapmakers draw the Earth as though its curved surface has been peeled off and opened out flat.

Filling the gaps

This is a peeled map. You can see a world map without gaps on pages 28–29.

The peeled map isn't much use because it has lots of gaps. Some parts have to be squashed or stretched to make a map without gaps.

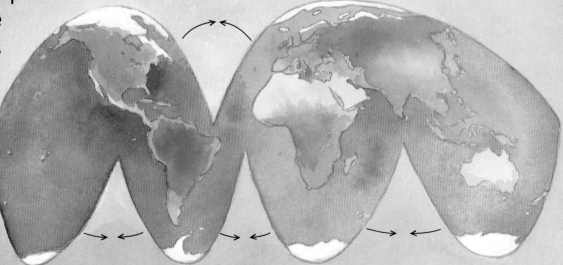

Countries and cities

There are more than 190 countries in the world. The place where one country meets another is called a border. On the maps in this book, the borders are shown as red dotted lines.

Borders

Many country borders are along rivers or mountains. Sometimes, borders are marked by fences or walls.

Some borders have gates where guards check who goes in and out.

Papua New Guinea has more than 700 islands like this.

Island groups

Some countries, such as Papua New Guinea, are made up of lots of islands. The maps in this book show their borders in the sea around the islands.

Can you find these things on the maps?

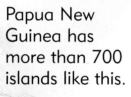
Big Ben

Parthenon

St. Basil's Cathedral

Forbidden City

Eiffel Tower

Big cities

Big cities can be very crowded. Many people work or live in tall buildings called skyscrapers. The black circles ● on the maps show where the biggest cities are.

Skyscrapers can fit many hundreds of people into a small space.

This is the White House, in Washington DC, USA. The President of the USA lives and works here.

Country capitals

The people in charge of a country work in a city called the capital. Lots of capitals have big, grand buildings. Capital cities are shown as black squares ■.

Street parties

In some cities, there are street parties called carnivals. People dress up and dance in the streets.

At carnivals, people wear bright, fancy costumes.

Blue Mosque

Winter Palace in St. Petersburg

Leaning Tower of Pisa

Sydney Opera House

Statue of Liberty

People

Millions and millions of people live around the world. In different parts of the world, people may look, talk and behave differently.

Japanese children wear kimonos for festivals and special occasions.

Dressing up

In some places, people dress up for special occasions in a style of clothes that people wore long ago. The clothes they wear are called traditional costumes.

Religions

A religion is a way of thinking about the world. Some people believe in one God and others believe in many gods. Most religions have holy places or buildings where people go to pray or think.

In Jerusalem, in Israel, there are many places where Christians, Muslims and Jewish people go to pray.

Can you find these people on the maps?

Guarani people

Zulu dancer

sitar player

rugby player

highland piper

Music and dancing

Many countries have their own styles of music and dancing. Some places have their own traditional musical instruments too.

Flamenco is a Spanish style of dancing to guitar music.

Chinese people often eat using chopsticks.

Eating

People around the world eat all kinds of foods. They also have many ways of cooking and eating. Food is transported long distances, so people can taste dishes from all around the world.

People from all around the world get together to play soccer.

Sharing interests

Although people can be very different, they also have lots in common. With travel, television, telephones and the Internet, it's easy for people to share ideas.

conga drummer

Tibetan monks

Hopi dancer

girl in a poncho

American football player

Getting around

There are many ways to get from one place to another. Journeys can be made by air, land or water. Some are quicker than others.

Jumbo jet planes can carry more than 600 people.

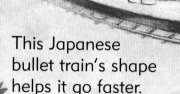

This Japanese bullet train's shape helps it go faster.

Long distances

Planes and trains can carry lots of people at a time. They make long journeys, at great speeds, all around the world.

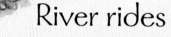

River rides

It is difficult to build roads in thick forests. The easiest way to travel there is along a river.

Many people canoe along the Amazon River.

Can you find these things on the maps?

basket boat

desert truck

traditional junk (boat)

Trans-Siberian Express

helicopter

Pedal power

In the busy city streets of India and China, many people use bicycles and rickshaws, instead of cars.

Rickshaws are pulled by people on foot or on bicycles. They are small, so they don't get stuck in traffic jams.

Children can ride on the back of a snowmobile.

Icy journeys

In snowy places, people use snowmobiles and sleds to get around. Snowmobiles have skis, instead of wheels, so they glide easily over the snow.

Watery city

A canal is a man-made river. In Venice, in Italy, there are canals instead of roads. People there use boats to get around the city.

Many people in Venice ride in boats called gondolas. They use poles to push the gondolas along.

Ice and snow

The white parts of the maps show places that are covered with ice and snow. The coldest places in the world are the Arctic in the north and Antarctica in the south.

The poles

The most northern place on Earth is called the North Pole. Whichever way you go from there is south. The South Pole is on the other side of the world.

Arctic terns spend half the year in the Arctic and the other half in Antarctica.

Poles apart

Penguins and polar bears never meet in the wild. This is because penguins live in Antarctica and polar bears only live in the Arctic.

Penguins huddle together to keep out the cold.

Polar bears have thick fur to keep them warm.

Can you find these things on the maps?

ice fish

humpback whale

American science station

Arctic fox

Saami people

These Inuit children are dressed in traditional parkas.

Keeping warm

People in frozen lands need to wrap up warm outside. Inuit people, who live in the Arctic, wear thick coats called parkas to keep out the cold.

Science in the snow

Antarctica is a large, cold island. There, scientists from all over the world work in science stations. They go there to study the weather and to find out about the animals that live there.

Scientists can measure how cold it is in the sky by fixing a thermometer to a weather balloon.

Icebreaker ships are strong and heavy. They break up the frozen ocean, clearing a way for other ships.

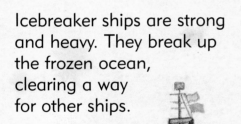

Frozen sea

There isn't any land at the North Pole, but much of the sea is frozen solid all year. In the summer, some of the ice melts and breaks up into huge chunks called icebergs.

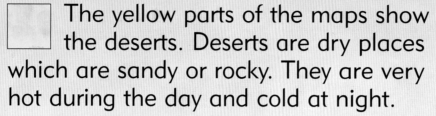

Deserts

The yellow parts of the maps show the deserts. Deserts are dry places which are sandy or rocky. They are very hot during the day and cold at night.

Flamingos flying over the Atacama Desert.

In sandy deserts, wind blows the sand into hills called dunes.

Desert records

The Sahara, in Africa, is the biggest, hottest desert in the world. The driest desert is the Atacama, in Chile. In parts, it hasn't rained for 400 years.

Oasis

An oasis is a place in the desert where there is water. Plants grow there and animals and people go there to drink.

These people are collecting water from an oasis.

Can you find these animals on the maps?

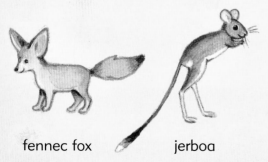

fennec fox   jerboa   blue-tongued skink   scorpion   rattlesnake

Thirsty animals

Camels can drink lots of water at once, then go for a week without any. They are suited to life in the desert in other ways too.

Camels can close their nostrils to stop sand from blowing in.

They have wide feet so they don't sink into the sand.

Desert people

Many desert people don't live in one place. They move around with their animals, to find water and food.

Plant survival

Desert plants have different ways of surviving in such dry places.

Many desert flowers only burst into bloom just after it rains.

Cactus plants store water in their stems.

Bedouins are desert people. Some of them live in camps like this.

Rivers and lakes

These people are using reed boats to cross Lake Titicaca.

 The dark blue lines and shading on the maps show where rivers and lakes are. The water in them comes from rain and melted snow. Many towns are built near rivers and lakes and lots of animals live in and near them.

A mountain lake

The highest lake in the world is Lake Titicaca, in South America. People there make boats from reeds that grow around the lake.

A river's journey

Rivers start high up in mountains, and flow downhill into lakes or the sea. The water slowly wears away the rock to make a dip in the ground, called a valley.

The Colorado River, in the USA, flows through the world's deepest valley. It is called the Grand Canyon.

A holy river

For many people, the Ganges River, in India, is a holy place. People from around the world go there to bathe in its water.

The water in a waterfall flows fast, and looks white and frothy.

People bathe in the Ganges River during religious festivals.

A waterfall

When a river flows over a steep step in the land, the water tumbles down it and makes a waterfall.

Muddy mouths

The wide, muddy place where a river joins the sea is called the river mouth. Lots of birds live there because the mud is full of plants and tiny fish to eat.

Crocodiles and herons live by the river mouth of the Nile, in Egypt.

Can you spot these things on the maps?

capybara   piranha   Caspian seal   hippopotamus   felucca boat

The world

The world is divided into seven large areas called continents. They are all named in big letters on this map.

The little pictures on this map show some world records.

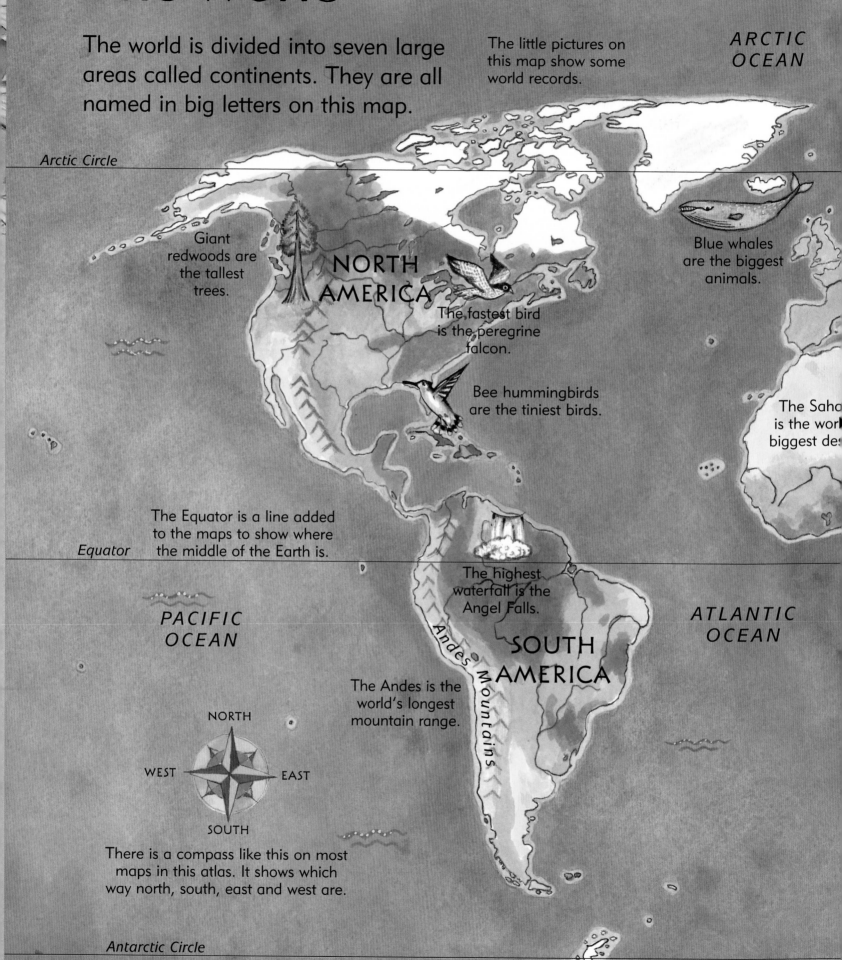

ARCTIC OCEAN

Arctic Circle

Giant redwoods are the tallest trees.

NORTH AMERICA

The fastest bird is the peregrine falcon.

Bee hummingbirds are the tiniest birds.

Blue whales are the biggest animals.

The Saha is the worl biggest des

The Equator is a line added to the maps to show where the middle of the Earth is.

Equator

The highest waterfall is the Angel Falls.

PACIFIC OCEAN

ATLANTIC OCEAN

Andes Mountains

SOUTH AMERICA

NORTH

WEST   EAST

SOUTH

The Andes is the world's longest mountain range.

There is a compass like this on most maps in this atlas. It shows which way north, south, east and west are.

Antarctic Circle

28

SOUTHERN OCEAN

The shading on the maps shows what the land is like in different parts of the world and where there are rivers, lakes, seas and oceans.

ice and snow   deserts   grasslands   forests   mountains   rivers and lakes   seas and oceans

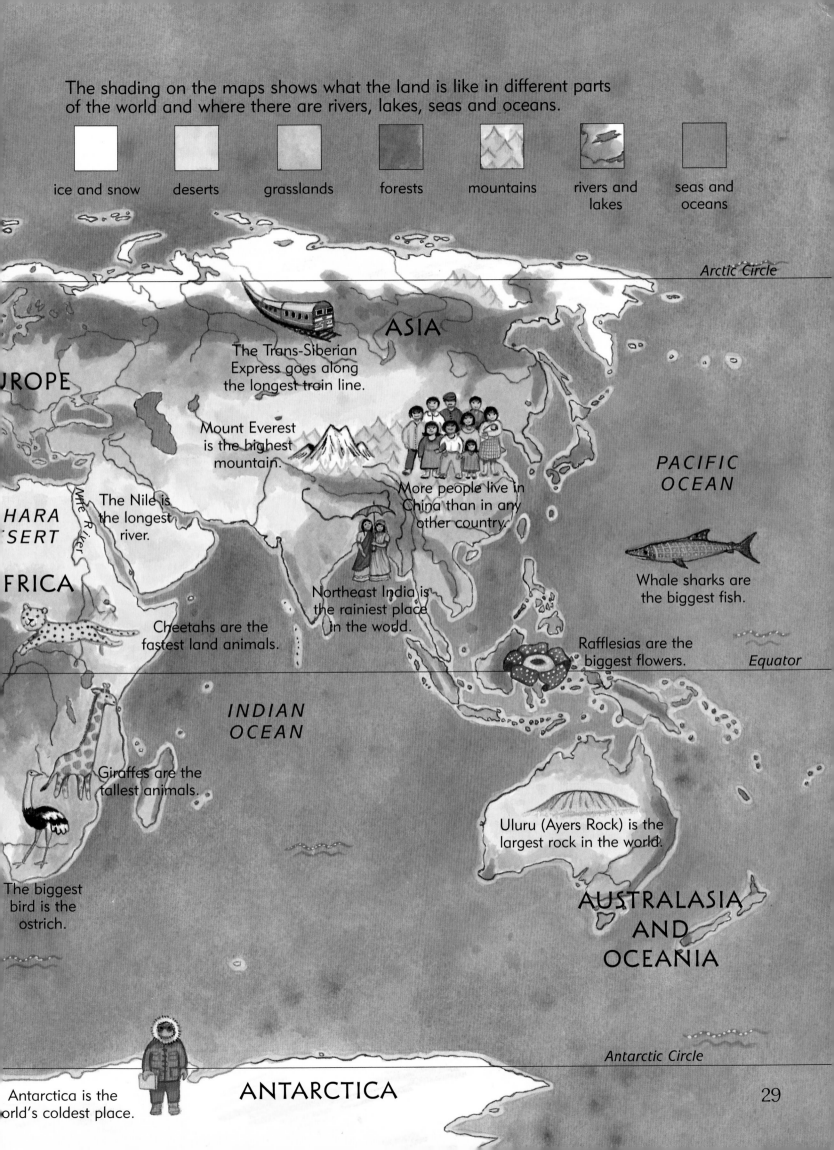

Arctic Circle

ASIA

The Trans-Siberian Express goes along the longest train line.

Mount Everest is the highest mountain.

EUROPE

More people live in China than in any other country.

PACIFIC OCEAN

Nile River

SAHARA DESERT

The Nile is the longest river.

AFRICA

Northeast India is the rainiest place in the world.

Whale sharks are the biggest fish.

Cheetahs are the fastest land animals.

Rafflesias are the biggest flowers.

Equator

INDIAN OCEAN

Giraffes are the tallest animals.

Uluru (Ayers Rock) is the largest rock in the world.

The biggest bird is the ostrich.

AUSTRALASIA AND OCEANIA

Antarctic Circle

Antarctica is the world's coldest place.

ANTARCTICA

29

North America

30

ARCTIC OCEAN

Arctic Circle

Greenland

Inuit people

Nuuk (Godthab)

minke whale

fishing boat

lobster

harp seal

cod

Canada goose

puffins

Labrador dog

cranberries

ptarmigan

igloo

snowy owl

Paper is made here.

maple tree

blue jay

harp seal cubs

boy in a kayak

beluga whale

Hudson Bay

cloudberries

The Great

Arctic terns

wolf

beaver

skunk

polar bear

Arctic hare

musk ox

moose

CANADA

combine harvester

icebreaker ship

husky dog

grizzly bear

mounted policeman

ice hockey player

Missouri River

arctic char

snow goose

muskrat

lumberjack (forester)

skier

bald eagle

Alaska (USA)

Rocky Mountains

traditional carved pole

Vancouver

Seattle

raccoon

snowmobile

caribou

walrus

Anchorage

Gulf of Alaska

Pacific salmon

PACIFIC OCEAN

Golden Gate bridge

killer whale

South America

Caribbean Sea

NORTH
EAST
WEST
SOUTH

Equator

white shark

oil rig

hummingbird

iguana

peccary

tapir

● Caracas

VENEZUELA

● Bogota

COLOMBIA

Quito ●

ECUADOR

fruit bat

scarlet
ibis

puma

Orinoco River

Angel Falls

cow

arrow
poison frog

jaguar

Coffee is
grown here.

brazil
nuts

condor

shrimps

rocket
base

Georgetown
■

GUYANA

Paramaribo
■

SURINAM

Cayenne
■

**FRENCH
GUIANA**

caiman

sloth

Amazon River

piranha

*Amazon
Rainforest*

spider
monkey

llama

Machu Picchu

Andes Mountains

Lima ■

PERU

reed boat
on Lake Titicaca

sardines

girl in
a poncho

cotton
plant

Gold is
mined here.

sugar
cane

Tocantins River

São Francisco River

bananas

conga
drummer

cocoa
beans

Coffee is
grown here.

lobster

capybara

armadillo

BRAZIL

anaconda

toucan

blue morpho
butterfly

parrot

Tapajós River

Madeira River

orchid

peanuts

spectacled
bear

La Paz ■

BOLIVIA

Sucre ■

Guarani
people

Brasilia Cathedral

■ Brasilia

Diamonds are
mined here.

ATLANTIC OCEAN

sardines

Rio de Janeiro

carnival dancers

oil tanker

São Paulo

oranges

surfer

sardines

The world

SOUTH AMERICA

This map shows where South America is.

mackerel

South Georgia

PARAGUAY

Asuncion

giant anteater

sheep ranches

Montevideo

URUGUAY

Buenos Aires

tango dancers

albatrosses

Falkland Islands

ARGENTINA

rhea

Paraná River

gaucho (cowboy)

sea lions

chinchilla

Atacama Desert

guanaco

Magellan penguin

Cape Horn

Andes Mountains

sheep

flamingos

pelican

CHILE

Santiago

grapes

monkey puzzle tree

rockhopper penguin

fur seal

PACIFIC OCEAN

fishing boat

southern right whale

mackerel

mackerel

killer whale

Australasia and Oceania

PACIFIC OCEAN

Northern
Mariana Islands

Moorish
idol

FEDERATED
STATES OF
MICRONESIA

PALAU

sea
cucumber

Equator

sacred
house

crowned
pigeon

tree
kangaroo

cuscus

dugong

PAPUA
NEW GUINEA

Port Moresby

box
jellyfish

coral

clown fish

pineapple
fish

Aboriginal
dancer

Great Barrier Reef

harlequin
fish

possum

butterfly
fish

spiny
anteater

koalas

frilled
lizard

dingo

boy
diving for
pearls

AUSTRALIA

Great Sandy Desert

kangaroos

blue-ringed
octopus

wallaby

Uluru
(Ayers Rock)

platypus

bottlenose
dolphin

grass
tree

thorny devil

Great Victoria
Desert

Opals are
mined here.

Darling River

Sydney
Opera
House

flying
doctor

wombat

sheep

parakeet

Sydney

Canberra

blue-tongued
skink

emu

black
swan

Melbourne

surfer

Perth

galah

Tasmania

sea dragon

crayfish

Tasmanian
devil

INDIAN
OCEAN

great white
shark

albatrosses

34

Hawaiian Islands

sea slug

girl wearing a garland

surfer

MARSHALL ISLANDS

jumbo jet plane

PACIFIC OCEAN

fairy terns

angel fish

cargo ship

NAURU

moray eel

blue shark

Equator

KIRIBATI

green turtles

flying fish

SOLOMON ISLANDS

parrot fish

TUVALU

Tokelau

manta rays

VANUATU

coconut palms

rugby player

Wallis and Futuna

SAMOA American Samoa

coconuts

fisherman in a canoe

bananas

tuna

French Polynesia

New Caledonia

FIJI

TONGA

Niue

sea horses

Cook Islands

bananas

Tahiti

swordfish

snappers

barracudas

giant squid

The world

kiwi

Maori dancer

NEW ZEALAND ■ Wellington

sperm whale

AUSTRALASIA AND OCEANIA

This map shows where Australasia and Oceania are.

sheep

hoki fish

Asia

Arctic Circle

herring

eider duck

fishing through ice

kittiwake

lynx

reindeer

Moscow

Ural Mountains

Volga River

noctule bat

flying squirrel

man in a fur hat

golden eagle

maize

honeybees

RUSSIA

Astana

saiga antelope

Blue Mosque

Black Sea

Caspian seal

Aral Sea

space agency

wheat

KAZAKHSTAN

bactrian camel

Istanbul

Ankara

skier

Caspian Sea

Bishkek

jerboa

Gobi Desert

GEORGIA

Turkish kebabs

ARMENIA

AZERBAIJAN

TURKEY

Tashkent

UZBEKISTAN

KYRGYZSTAN

Cyprus

SYRIA

TURKMENISTAN

TAJIKISTAN

snow leopard

Great Wall of China

rug

Ashgabat

LEBANON

jackal

ISRAEL

Damascus

IRAQ

Tehran

AFGHANISTAN

Tibetan monks

Jerusalem

Baghdad

Kabul

The Himalayas

Mount Everest

yak

JORDAN

IRAN

Islamabad

New Delhi

NEPAL

hyena

KUWAIT

date palms

Afghan hound

PAKISTAN

Indus River

Kathmandu

Ganges River

BHUTAN

oil well

QATAR

Bedouin people

UNITED ARAB EMIRATES

Muscat

Taj Mahal in Agra

BANGLADESH

boy on an elephant

Mecca

Riyadh

water towers

SAUDI ARABIA

OMAN

sitar player

INDIA

Dhaka

Red Sea

Arabian horse

girl in a sari

Bengal tiger

BURMA

Sana

Arabian camel

Bombay

rickshaw

Rangoon

YEMEN

Arabian Sea

Andaman Islands

Bangkok

Socotra

orchid

NORTH

sacred cow

tea plant

floating market

WEST

EAST

Arabian fishing boats

Sri Jayewardenepura Kotte

SRI LANKA

SOUTH

Colombo

Kuala Lumpur

Equator

oil tanker

Maldives

coral reef

rhinoceros

soldier fish

INDIAN OCEAN

tiger shark

snappers

36

beluga whale

narwhal

polar bears

ringed seal

walrus

lemming

snow goose

Lena River

snowmobile

bearded seal

Bering Sea

giant kelp forest

bowhead whales

brown bear

Siberian tiger

Sea of Okhotsk

sea lion

fishing boat

wild mushrooms

Trans-Siberian Express

sperm whale

pollock

ger (tent)

Kites are made here.

crested puffin

girl in a kimono

PACIFIC OCEAN

Ulan Bator

NGOLIA

Forbidden City

Vladivostock

NORTH KOREA

bullet train

puffer fish

white-sided dolphin

Beijing

Pyongyang

JAPAN

erracotta Army

Yellow River

Seoul

SOUTH KOREA

Tokyo

CHINA

rice plants

crane

sumo wrestler

Yangtze River

iant nda

bamboo

pagoda

traditional junk (boat)

Taipei

octopus

TAIWAN

The world

TNAM

Hanoi

Hong Kong

South China Sea

dugong

Philippine Sea

ASIA

entiane

ILAND

Manila

basket boat

THE PHILIPPINES

manta ray

This map shows where Asia is.

BODIA

nom enh

pineapples

AYSIA

BRUNEI

Borneo

giant clam

GAPORE

Celebes

Equator

atra

orang-utan

rafflesia flower

coconut palms

cowrie shells

rubber trees

INDONESIA

Jakarta

Java

EAST TIMOR

New Guinea

temple

Arafura Sea

Africa

Mediterranean Sea

Madeira

Rabat ■

lemons

■ Algiers

■ Tunis

TUNISIA

Tripoli ■

olives

Atlas Mountains

MOROCCO

Canary Islands

Laayoune ■

WESTERN
SAHARA

*ATLANTIC
OCEAN*

ground
squirrel

Berber
people

oasis

spices

LIBYA

desert truck

ALGERIA

Sahara Desert

date
palm

bottlenose
dolphin

fisherman

MAURITANIA

■ Nouakchott

MALI

Niger River

camel train

scorpion

NIGER

gerb

CAPE VERDE
ISLANDS

SENEGAL

■ Dakar

baboon

hippopotamus

round
houses

CHA

Ndjame ■

THE GAMBIA

GUINEA-BISSAU

GUINEA

Bamako ■

BURKINA
FASO

Niamey ■

Conakry ■

Freetown ■

bananas

cocoa beans

BENIN

TOGO

Abuja ■

NIGERIA

Lagos ●

bee-eater

SIERRA LEONE

Monrovia ■

LIBERIA

Yamoussoukro ■

IVORY
COAST

Accra ■

GHANA

Yaounde ■

Bangu

CAMEROON

cargo ship

conger eel

Equator

EQUATORIAL
GUINEA

Libreville ■

GABON

CONGO

Brazza

ATLANTIC OCEAN

chimpanzee

Kinsh

ANGOLA

Luanda ■

flying fish

oryx

The world

cruise ship

meerkats

anchovies

NAMI

Windhoek

AFRICA

This map shows where Africa is.

great white
shark

ost

Cap
Tow

38

fishing boat

Cairo

well
pyramids
EGYPT

felucca
boat

nnec
ox

gourd

Nile River

Red Sea

*Nubian
Desert*

crocodile

ERITREA

Khartoum
Asmara

SUDAN

ETHIOPIA

Addis
Ababa

DJIBOUTI

tortoise

acacia
tree

NTRAL
RICAN
UBLIC

sugar
cane

rhinoceros

lobelia

hoopoe

SOMALIA

Arab fishing
boats

*INDIAN
OCEAN*

NORTH

DEMOCRATIC
PUBLIC OF THE
CONGO

UGANDA

zebra

coconut
palms

WEST   EAST

Kampala

*Lake
Victoria*

KENYA

coffee
beans

Mogadishu

SOUTH

Congo River

gorilla

RWANDA

BURUNDI

TANZANIA

Nairobi

lion

Zanzibar
butterfly fish

frigate bird

Equator

cow fish

mandrill

Dodoma

Dar es Salaam

SEYCHELLES

hammerhead
shark

vulture

cheetah

African
elephant

cloves

oriental
sweetlips fish

MALAWI

ZAMBIA

Lilongwe

Lusaka

Zambezi River

aye-aye

ffe

Harare

aardvark

baobab
tree

Antananarivo

octopus

ZIMBABWE

Victoria Falls

MOZAMBIQUE

MADAGASCAR

MAURITIUS

OTSWANA
*lahari
esert*

orone

sunbird

Pretoria

nnesburg

ring-tailed
lemur

emfontein
Zulu dancer

Maputo

SWAZILAND

LESOTHO

**SOUTH
AFRICA**

jellyfish

pes

39

Europe

ARCTIC OCEAN

Arctic Circle

killer whale

ICELAND

Reykjavik ■

hot mud pool

ATLANTIC OCEAN

humpback whale

cod

Faroe Islands

blue whale

oil rig

skier

NORWAY

Oslo ■

fjord

NORTH

WEST

EAST

SOUTH

fishing boat

salmon

Shetland Islands

highland piper

wooden church

gannets

DENMARK

Copenhagen ■

Irish dancer

UNITED KINGDOM

North Sea

pig

wind f

Dublin ■

IRELAND

sheep

NETHERLANDS

Amsterdam ■

Big Ben

Stonehenge

London ■

The Hague ■

Cars are made here

Be

cargo ship

ferry

Eden project

Brussels ■

BELGIUM

LUXEMBOURG

GERMANY

Pragu

Paris ■

Eiffel Tower

grapes

castle

Bern ■

AUST

mussels

apples

FRANCE

SWITZERLAND

oysters

Bay of Biscay

croissants

lavender

skier

The Alps

ITALY

SLOV

PORTUGAL

art gallery in Bilbao

church in Barcelona

skier

Leaning Tower of Pisa

gond in Ve

Belem Tower

Madrid ■

cruise ship

Corsica

Rom ■

Lisbon ■

SPAIN

bull fighter

swordfish

cork oak tree

Sardinia

St Peter' the Vatic

Madeira

oranges

flamenco dancer

Balearic Islands

sardines

grapes

Sicily

vol

Mediterranean Sea

Canary Islands

MA

Arctic hare

capercaillie

fishing through ice

Ural Mountains

Siberian chipmunk

flounder

puffins

Saami people

reindeer

wolverine

sparrow hawk

Ural owl

WEDEN

wild mushrooms

lynx

sable

ballet dancers

wheat

FINLAND

Paper is made here.

beaver

RUSSIA

oose

Baltic Sea

gymnast

wild horses

Helsinki

Winter Palace in St. Petersburg

Moscow

maize

Stockholm

Tallinn

ESTONIA

St. Basil's Cathedral

Volga River

sprats

LATVIA

Riga

red fox

COW

black stork

LITHUANIA

potatoes

Russian dolls

Vilnius

Ships are made here.

Minsk

BELARUS

wild boar

Cossack dancer

balalaika player

Caspian Sea

POLAND

Warsaw

deer

Kiev

Dnieper River

Don River

uropean bison

brown bear

chamois

UKRAINE

ECH UBLIC

Carpathian Mountains

MOLDOVA

sunflowers

The world

enna

Bratislava

Chisinau

Budapest

castle

space telescope

EUROPE

HUNGARY

ROMANIA

OATIA

Belgrade

Bucharest

OSNIA & ZEGOVINA

Danube River

Black Sea

sturgeon

djevo

SERBIA & MONTENEGRO

BULGARIA

fortress in Dubrovnik

Sofia

grapes

Tirana

MACEDONIA

TURKEY

Istanbul

This map shows where Europe is.

ALBANIA

olives

GREECE

Athens

Parthenon

olives

Crete

fishing boat

41

The Arctic

Bering Sea

Gulf of Alaska

fishing boat

volcanoes

Sea of Okhotsk

walrus

bearded seal

snowmobile

Alaska (USA)

Chukchi tent

husky racer

Chukchi Sea

Wrangel Island

purple heron

Siberian tiger

moose

wolf

Arctic loon

RUSSIA

CANADA

polar bear

Beaufort Sea

New Siberia Islands

ARCTIC OCEAN

Laptev Sea

snowy owl

salmon

narwhal

lynx

Canada goose

Arctic fox

Arctic terns

helicopter

Severnaya Zemlya

lemming

stoat

Arctic hare

North Pole

Kara Sea

Ellesmere Island

ringed seal

explorer

Baffin Island

Franz Josef Land

Novaya Zemlya

Arctic poppies

caribou

polar bear

Arctic chars

harp seal

satellite station

GREENLAND

Svalbard

Barents Sea

Arctic Circle

boy in a kayak

Nuuk (Godthab)

minke whale

musk ox

ptarmigan

puffins

cod

Reykjavik

ICELAND

The world

THE ARCTIC

ANTARCTICA

The Arctic and Antarctica are on opposite sides of the world.

ATLANTIC OCEAN

ferry

fishing boat

42

Antarctica

South Georgia

ATLANTIC OCEAN

SOUTHERN OCEAN

Africa is this way.

sea bass

blue whale

krill

snail fish

INDIAN OCEAN

wandering albatrosses

cruise ship

Weddell Sea

robot submarine

macaroni penguin

scientist with a weather balloon

British science station

Adelie penguins

Antarctic Peninsula

leopard seal

Ronne Ice Shelf

South America is this way.

ANTARCTICA

fur seal

Weddell seal

rockhopper penguin

chinstrap penguin

American science station

South Pole

caterpillar truck

brittle star

Antarctic Circle

gentoo penguins

snowmobile

Transantarctic Mountains

ski plane

elephant seal

Ross Ice Shelf

Australian science station

Ross Sea

emperor penguins

king penguin

French science station

giant petrels

ice fish

soft coral

blue-eyed shag

cod

krill

krill

PACIFIC OCEAN

porbeagle shark

SOUTHERN OCEAN

killer whale

Arctic terns

Australia is this way.

43

A trip around the world

Are you ready for a trip around the world?
Look back through this book and try this
fun quiz to find out. The answers
are all on page 48.

Packing your bags

You'll need to pack
carefully for your trip.
Can you match
these things to the
places where
you'll need them?

1. Climbing boots
2. A warm coat
3. A water bottle
4. A diving suit

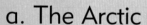

a. The Arctic
b. Mount Everest
c. The Atacama Desert
d. The Great Barrier Reef

Things to see

1. Would you see
penguins in the Arctic or
in Antarctica?

2. In which town in Italy
would you see canals
instead of roads?

3. Which is the only
country where you can
see koalas and
kangaroos in the wild?

4. Which city in Brazil
would you visit to see
people dressed up for
a carnival?

Country shapes

Here are the shapes of some of the countries you might visit. Can you recognize them from the maps?

4.

1.

2.

3.

Blue clues

Can you find and name all of these things with "blue" in their names?

1. A butterfly that lives in the Amazon rainforest.

2. An octopus that swims near Australia.

3. An Australian lizard with an unusual tongue.

4. A North American bird.

People to meet

In which countries would you expect to meet these people?

1. Hopi dancer
2. Girl in a kimono
3. Reggae singer
4. Zulu dancer

Index of places

Index of things

Answers

Things to spot

Countries and cities
Big Ben, 40
Parthenon, 41
St. Basil's Cathedral, 41
Forbidden City, 37
Eiffel Tower, 40
Blue Mosque, 36
Winter Palace in St. Petersburg, 41
Leaning Tower of Pisa, 40
Sydney Opera House, 34
Statue of Liberty, 31

People
Guarani people, 32
Zulu dancer, 39
sitar player, 36
rugby player, 35
highland piper, 40
conga drummer, 32
Tibetan monks, 36
Hopi dancer, 31
girl in a poncho, 32
American football player, 31

Getting around
basket boat, 37
desert truck, 38
traditional junk (boat), 37
Trans-Siberian Express, 29, 37
helicopter, 42

Ice and snow
ice fish, 43
humpback whale, 40
American science station, 43
Arctic fox, 42
Saami people, 41

Deserts
fennec fox, 39
jerboa, 36
blue-tongued skink, 34
scorpion, 38
rattlesnake, 31

Grasslands
kangaroos, 34
guanaco, 33
buffalo, 30
giraffe, 39
meerkats, 38

lion, 39
giant anteater, 33
African elephant, 39
oryx, 38
rhea, 33

Forests
blue morpho butterfly, 32
armadillo, 32
red fox, 41
raccoon, 30
anaconda, 32
grizzly bear, 30
wild mushrooms, 37
lumberjack (forester), 30
chimpanzee, 38
toucan, 32

Mountains
bald eagle, 30
Mount Everest, 29, 36
yak, 36
chamois, 41
Ural owl, 41

Rivers and lakes
capybara, 32
piranha, 32

Caspian seal, 36
hippopotamus, 38
felucca boat, 39

Seas and oceans
red snappers, 31
butterfly fish, 34
green turtles, 35
scuba diver, 31
seahorses, 35
common dolphins, 31
marlin, 31
giant squid, 35
shrimps, 32
blue shark, 35

A trip around the world

Packing your bags
1. b. You'll need climbing boots on Mount Everest.
2. a. A warm coat will keep out the cold in the Arctic.
3. c. The Atacama Desert is the driest place on Earth, so you'll need a water bottle.
4. d. You'll need a diving suit to dive down to the Great Barrier Reef.

Places to see
1. Antarctica
2. Venice
3. Australia
4. Rio de Janeiro

Country shapes
1. New Zealand
2. Mexico
3. Australia
4. Italy

Blue clues
1. Blue morpho butterfly
2. Blue-ringed octopus
3. Blue-tongued skink
4. Blue jay

People to meet
1. USA
2. Japan
3. Jamaica
4. South Africa

Managing editor: Gillian Doherty   Managing designer: Russell Punter
The publishers are grateful to the following organizations and individuals for their permission to reproduce material. **p6** This image is an extract from the Millennium Map™ which is © getmapping.com plc; **p7** ©Tom Van Sant, Geosphere Project/Planetary Visions/Science Photo Library